At the Bakery

Illustrations

Penny Dann

Picture Credits

© Bruno De Hogues/Tony Stone Images: cover
© Gregg Andersen/Gallery 19: 4, 6, 8, 10, 12, 14, 16, 18, 20, 22, 24, 26, 28, 30
© Jack McConnell: 3

Library of Congress Cataloging-in-Publication Data

Greene, Carol.

At the bakery / by Carol Greene.
p.   cm.
Summary: Describes, in simple text, what happens
at a bakery, the people who work there,
and some of the special machines
that are used for making breads and cakes.
ISBN 1-56766-563-2 (library reinforced : alk. paper)
1. Bakers and bakeries—Juvenile literature.
[1. Bakers and bakeries.]   I. Title.

TX763.G652   1998   98-3109
664'.02—dc21   CIP
                            AC

At the Bakery

By Carol Greene

The Child's World®, Inc.

Bakeries come in many sizes.
This is a big one.

MMMM!

The things that are baked
here make the neighborhood
smell good.

CLANK! THUNK! WHIRR!

Bakers use lots of different machines. Machines make their job easier. They help the bakers make lots of things quickly.

Bakers wear special clothes so the things they are making stay nice and clean.

FLOP! FLOP!

This machine mixes flour, eggs, and other **ingredients**. When everything is mixed together, the baker stops the machine. He takes the thick mixture out of the bowl.

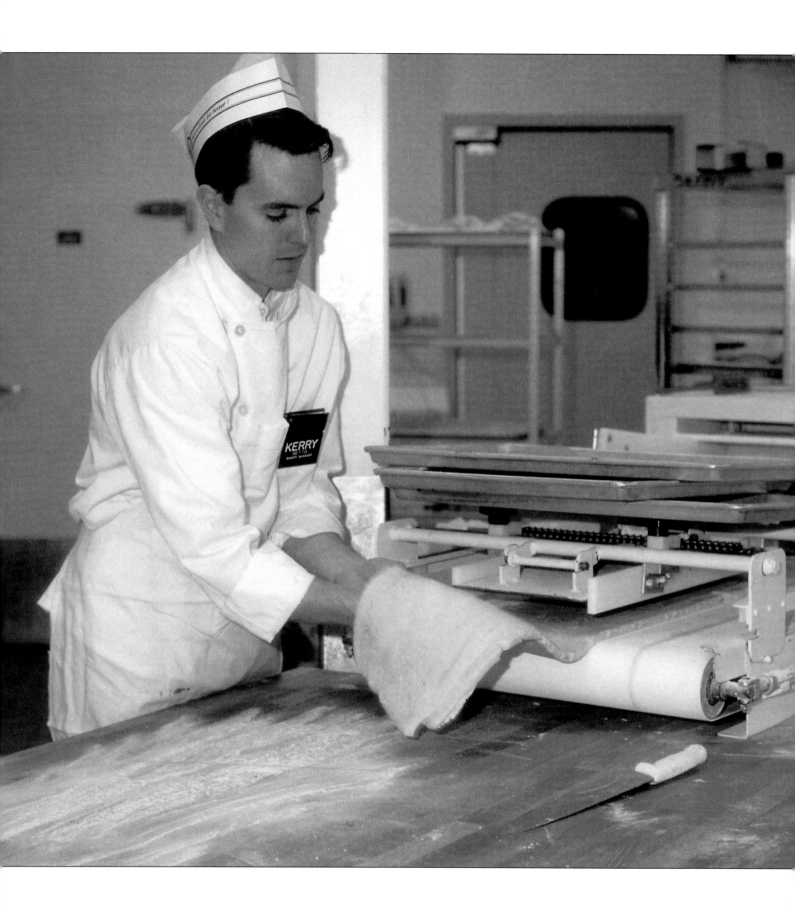

SQUEAK! HUMMM!

The thick mixture is now called **dough**. The baker wants to use the dough to make rolls. First, he must use a machine to flatten it.

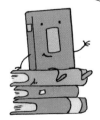

The baker watches the machine closely. He makes sure it is working right.

CHOP! PAT!

Now the bakers cut the dough into strips. They twist the strips and roll them up.

Rolls can be made into lots of different shapes. These are shaped like swirls.

These bakers are making bread. First they make some dough in the mixer. When it is ready, they cut the dough into small pieces. They shape the dough into **loaves**. Then each loaf goes into a pan.

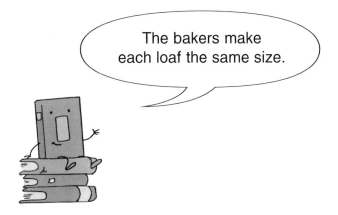

The bakers make each loaf the same size.

THUNK! THUNK!

Bakers called oven tenders put the loaf pans into a big oven. After the bread is baked, the tenders let the loaves cool on racks. Then they turn the pans over and take the loaves out.

Other bakers are busy making cake **batter**. They use the huge mixers to blend lots of ingredients. They can make cakes in all kinds of flavors.

This huge bowl is full of thick cake batter.

PLOP! PLOP!

When the batter is ready, the baker puts it into pans. He puts fruit on top of each cake. Then the cakes are ready to go into the oven.

The baker gives the cakes to an oven tender. Then he goes back to his area. It is time to make more cakes!

Sometimes people want to have a special cake made for them. Then the cake goes to the decorating area. Here bakers use icing and candies to make the cake look nice.

Decorators can make cookies and cupcakes look nice, too.

HISSS!

Cake decorators use lots of different tools. Some use bags to squirt sticky icing. Others use machines to spray icing in different colors.

This decorator is going to use a spray machine to color this cake.

FZZZ! FZZZ!

This baker is busy with another cake. She writes on it. She makes pretty swirls. She draws nice pictures, too.

Working with icing takes a lot of practice.

The baker is finished. She has done a beautiful job. It's a birthday cake for a little girl!

GLOSSARY

batter (BA–ter)
Batter is a thick mixture made with eggs, flour, and milk. When it is baked, the batter turns into cake or cookies.

dough (DOH)
Dough is a thick, sticky mixture of flour and water or milk. Baking dough turns it into bread.

ingredients (in–GREE–dee–ents)
Ingredients are the things go into a mixture. Bakers use lots of different ingredients.

loaves (LOHVZ)
Bakers often form dough into shapes called loaves. Many loaves are round.

machines (muh–SHEENZ)
Machines are tools that help people do things. Bakers use many different machines.

INDEX

CAROLE GREENE has published over 200 books for children. She also likes to read books, make teddy bears, work in her garden, and sing. Ms. Greene lives in Webster Groves, Missouri.